ANIMAL BATTLES

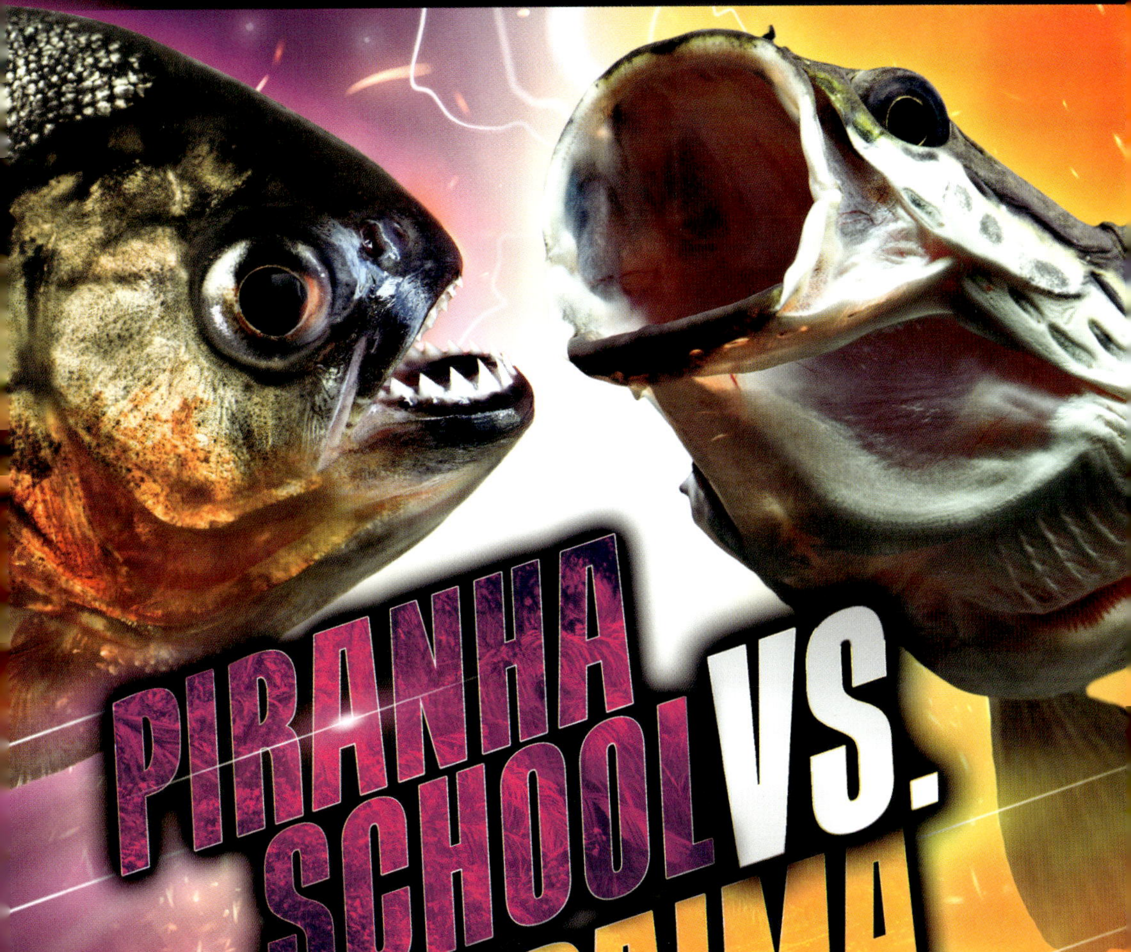

PIRANHA SCHOOL VS. ARAPAIMA

BY NATHAN SOMMER

TORQUE™

BELLWETHER MEDIA • MINNEAPOLIS, MN

Torque brims with excitement perfect for thrill-seekers of all kinds. Discover daring survival skills, explore uncharted worlds, and marvel at mighty engines and extreme sports. In *Torque* books, anything can happen. Are you ready?

This edition first published in 2025 by Bellwether Media, Inc.

Library of Congress Cataloging-in-Publication Data

LC record for Piranha School vs. Arapaima available at: https://lccn.loc.gov/2024036211

Editor: Suzane Nguyen Designer: Hunter Demmin

Printed in the United States of America, North Mankato, MN.

TABLE OF CONTENTS

THE COMPETITORS

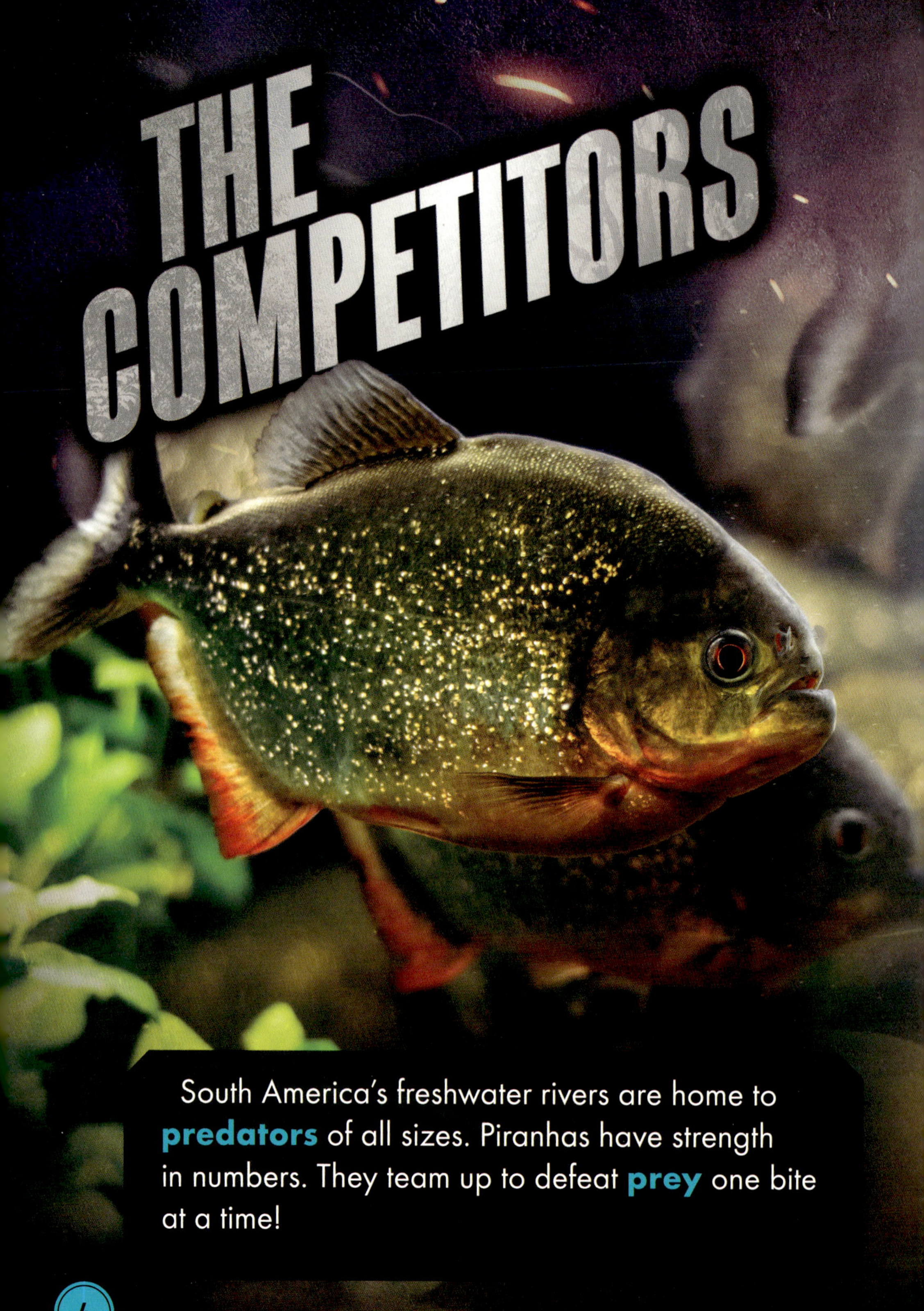

South America's freshwater rivers are home to **predators** of all sizes. Piranhas have strength in numbers. They team up to defeat **prey** one bite at a time!

Piranhas share their **habitats** with beastly arapaimas. Arapaimas hunt any prey they can suck into their mouths. Which predator rules the rivers?

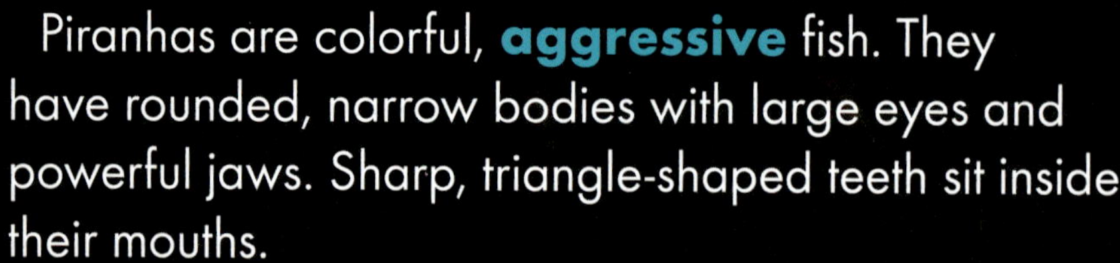

Piranhas are colorful, **aggressive** fish. They have rounded, narrow bodies with large eyes and powerful jaws. Sharp, triangle-shaped teeth sit inside their mouths.

Piranhas are **omnivores**. They are found throughout South America's lakes and rivers. The fish live and hunt in groups called schools. These schools can sometimes have more than 100 members!

RED-BELLIED PIRANHA PROFILE

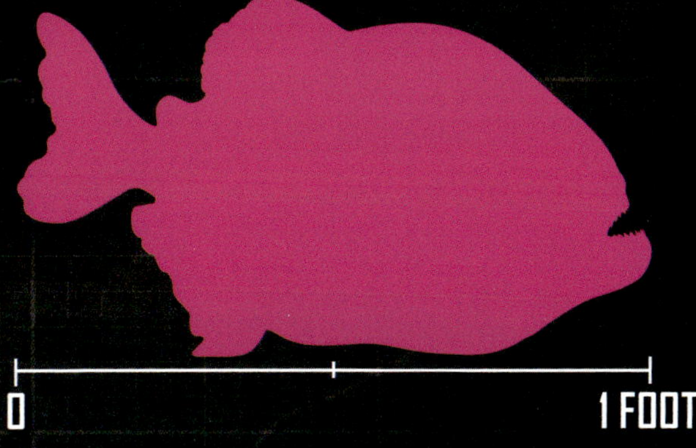

LENGTH

OVER 1 FOOT
(0.3 METERS)

WEIGHT

UP TO 4 POUNDS
(1.8 KILOGRAMS)

HABITATS

RIVERS

LAKES

RED-BELLIED PIRANHA RANGE

ARAPAIMA PROFILE

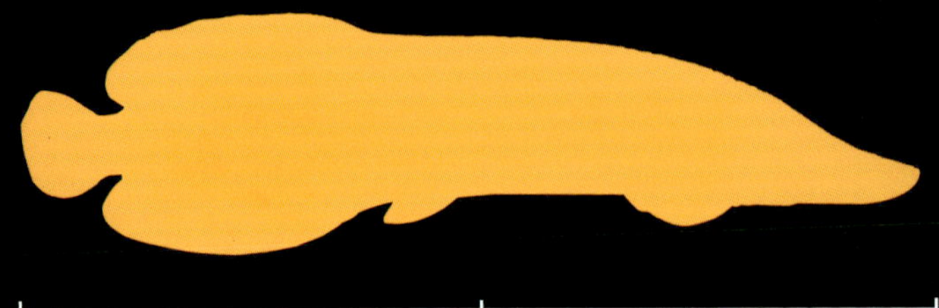

0 | 5 FEET | 10 FEET

LENGTH
UP TO 10 FEET (3 METERS)

WEIGHT
UP TO 440 POUNDS (200 KILOGRAMS)

HABITATS

RIVERS

LAKES

STREAMS

ARAPAIMA RANGE

RANGE

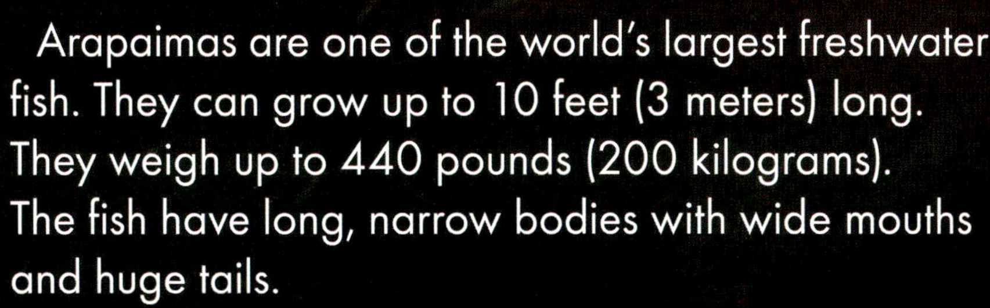

Arapaimas are one of the world's largest freshwater fish. They can grow up to 10 feet (3 meters) long. They weigh up to 440 pounds (200 kilograms). The fish have long, narrow bodies with wide mouths and huge tails.

Arapaimas live in waters near South America's Amazon River. The fish prefer warm, shallow water.

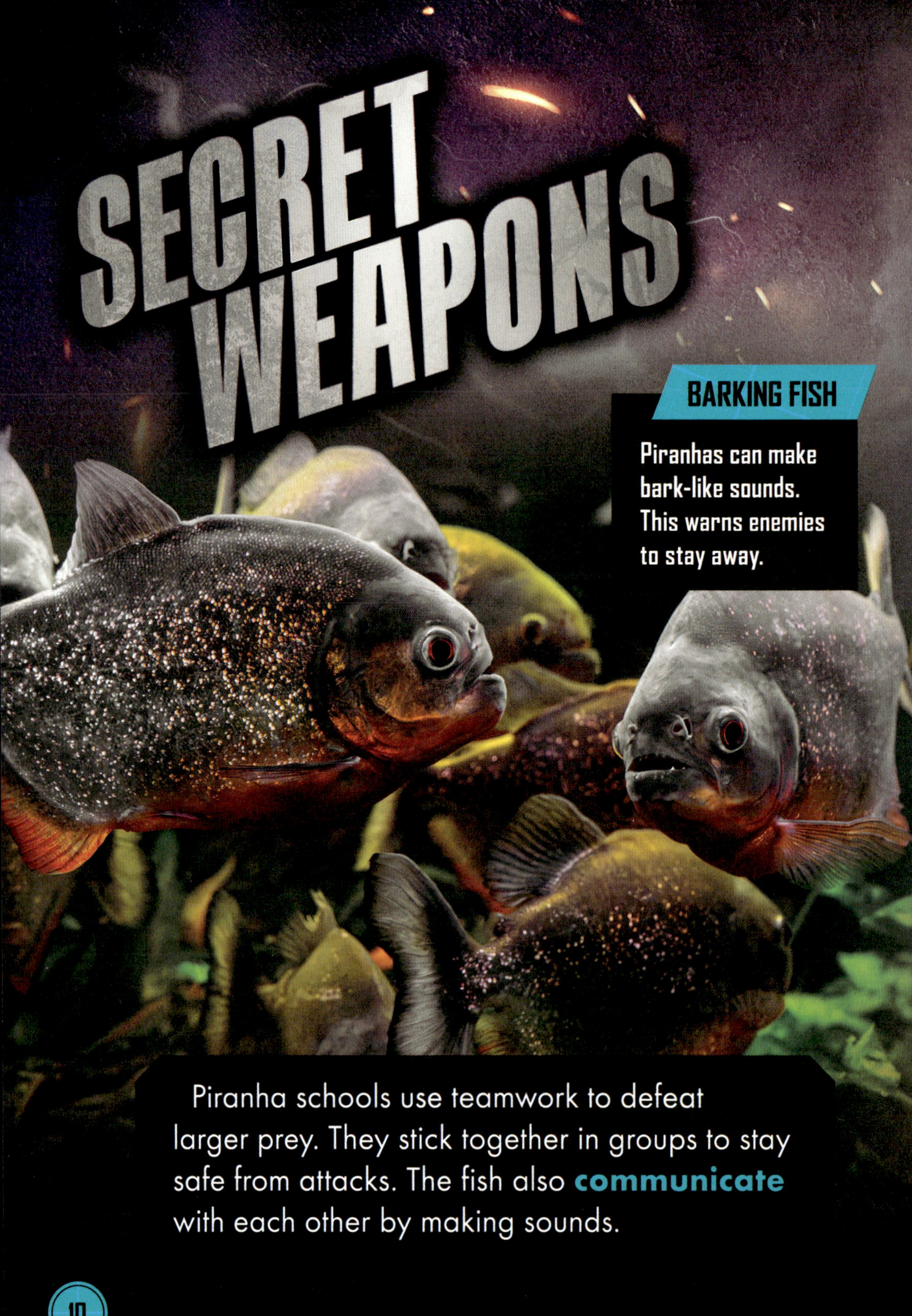

SECRET WEAPONS

BARKING FISH

Piranhas can make bark-like sounds. This warns enemies to stay away.

Piranha schools use teamwork to defeat larger prey. They stick together in groups to stay safe from attacks. The fish also **communicate** with each other by making sounds.

Arapaimas have thick scales. The scales cover their whole bodies. They are hard to break. These keep the fish safe from enemies that bite.

FISH OUT OF WATER

Arapaimas breathe air. They can survive out of water for up to 24 hours.

SECRET WEAPONS

PIRANHA SCHOOL

TEAMWORK

SENSE OF SMELL

POWERFUL JAWS

Piranhas have an excellent sense of smell. They can smell blood in the water from miles away. The fish can sense live and **scavenged** prey. This helps them find their next meal.

SECRET WEAPONS

ARAPAIMA

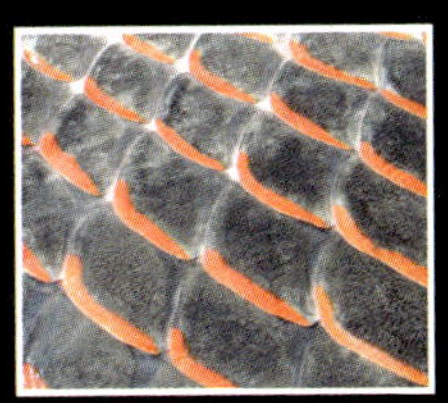
SCALES

WIDE MOUTHS

BONY TONGUES

Arapaimas use their wide mouths like vacuums. They open them wide to suck in prey. Most small prey cannot escape their powerful gulps!

PIRANHA TOOTH

0.16 INCHES (0.4 CENTIMETERS)

PIRANHA VS. HUMAN

Piranhas do not often bite people. But their attacks on humans can be deadly!

Piranhas use powerful jaws to sink their razor-sharp teeth into prey. The fish have a bite **force** of more than 30 times their body weight. Their bites are strong enough to break bones!

Arapaimas have large, bony tongues. They use these to crush prey. The tongues also have teeth on them. They shred meat off prey.

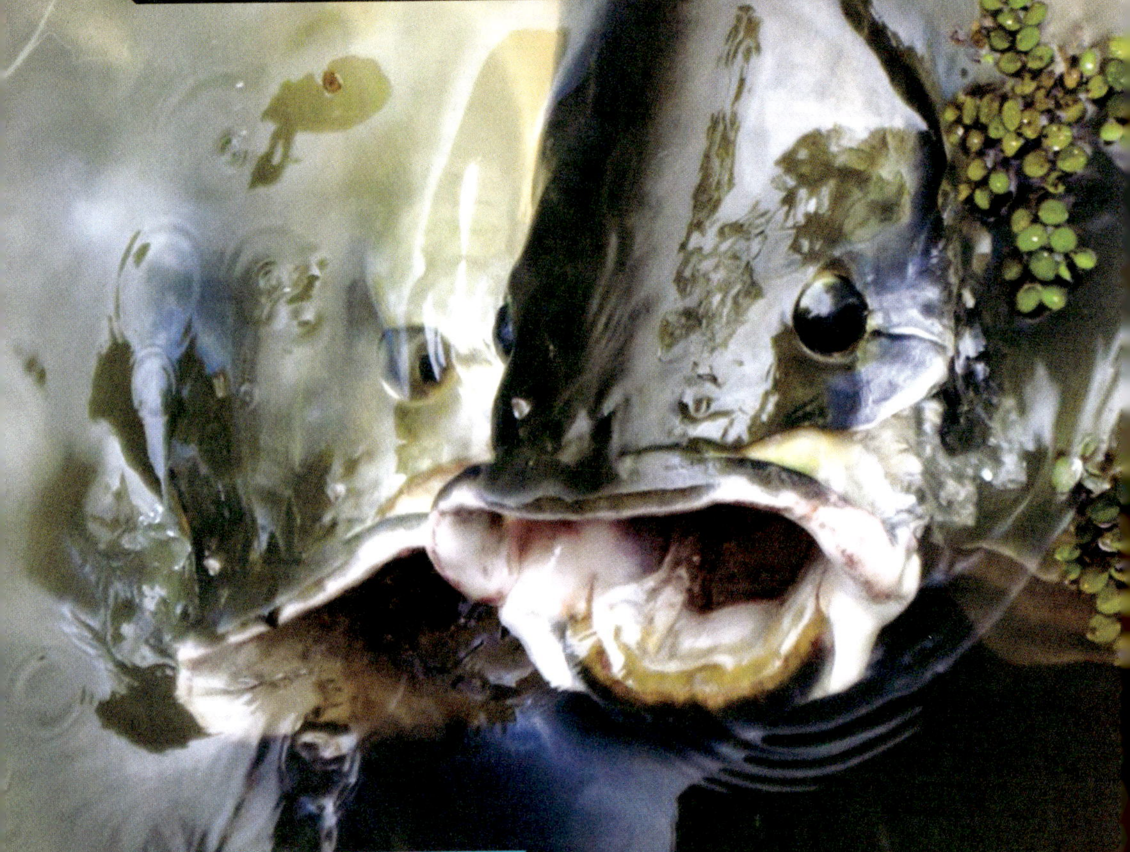

SIZE COMPARISON

ARAPAIMA
10 FEET
(3 METERS)
0
5 FEET
10 FEET
CAR
14.7 FEET
(4.5 METERS)
0
5 FEET
10 FEET
15 FEET

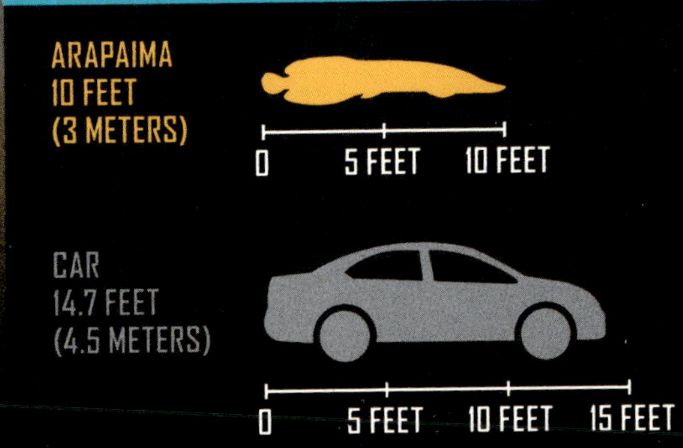

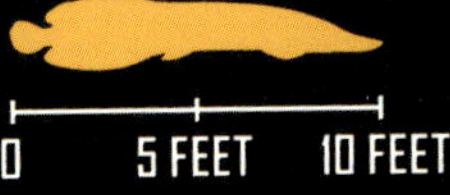

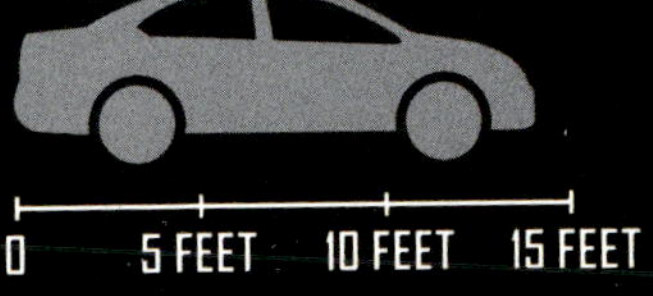

ATTACK MOVES

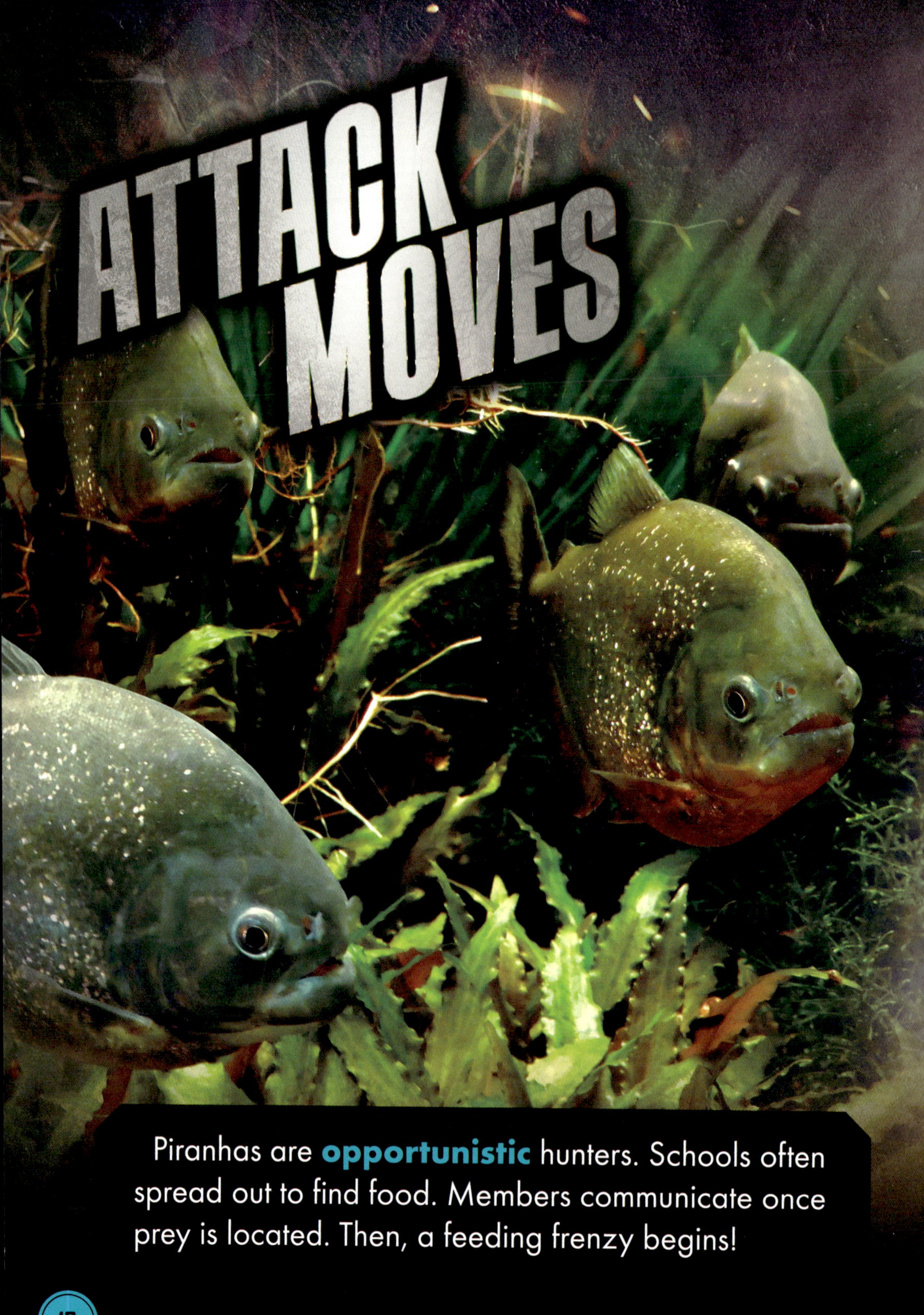

Piranhas are **opportunistic** hunters. Schools often spread out to find food. Members communicate once prey is located. Then, a feeding frenzy begins!

Arapaimas hunt by gulping. When prey is close, they open their mouth to suck in everything nearby! Then they defeat it with their sharp tongues and teeth.

Piranhas take turns quickly biting chunks out of prey. They often bite smaller prey in the fins and tail. Schools usually only attack larger prey that are already dead or injured.

TAKE A BREATH

Arapaimas must surface for air every 10 to 20 minutes.

Arapaimas also hunt above the surface! They use bursts of speed to leap out of the water. They can capture birds and small **mammals** from nearby tree branches.

READY, FIGHT!

A piranha school approaches a resting arapaima. They think it is injured. The school begins biting the arapaima. This wakes it up! It quickly fights back.

The arapaima opens its mouth to gulp a few piranhas. It uses its bony tongue to shred them. This scares the school away. The group attack against the arapaima failed today!

GLOSSARY

aggressive—ready to fight

communicate—to share thoughts and feelings using sounds, faces, and actions

force—the strength of an action

habitats—homes or areas where animals prefer to live

mammals—warm-blooded animals that have backbones and feed their young milk

omnivores—animals that eat both plants and animals

opportunistic—taking advantage of a situation

predators—animals that hunt other animals for food

prey—animals that are hunted by other animals for food

scavenged—related to food that is already dead

TO LEARN MORE

AT THE LIBRARY

Clasky, Leonard. *20 Things You Didn't Know About Piranhas.* Buffalo, N.Y.: PowerKids Press, 2024.

Coppolino, Marla. *Beaver vs. Piranha.* Mankato, Minn.: Black Rabbit Books, 2022.

Mattern, Joanne. *Arapaimas.* Minneapolis, Minn.: Bellwether Media, 2024.

ON THE WEB

FACTSURFER

Factsurfer.com gives you a safe, fun way to find more information.

1. Go to www.factsurfer.com
2. Enter "piranha school vs. arapaima" into the search box and click 🔍.
3. Select your book cover to see a list of related content.

INDEX

The images in this book are reproduced through the courtesy of: Eric Isselee, front cover (piranha); guentermanaus, front cover (piranha), p. 12 (powerful jaws); Ammit Jack, front cover (arapaima), p. 13 (wide mouths); Aleron Val, p. 4; SergioRocha, p. 5; Hayati Kayhan, pp. 6-7; N-sky, pp. 8-9; Katerina Maksymenko, p. 10; TatianaMironenko/ Getty, pp. 11, 13; mr_tigga, p. 12; Boris Bulychev, p. 12 (teamwork); nounours, p. 12 (sense of smell); Fabio Maffei, p. 13 (scales); juerginho, p. 13 (bony tongues); Sylvain Cordier/ Getty, p. 14; Matyas Rehak, p. 15; E-lona, p. 16; William2023, p. 17; John Madere/ Getty, p. 18; YASUYOSHI CHIBA/ Getty, p. 19; Leonid Serebrennikov/ Alamy, pp. 20-21; WildStrawberry, pp. 20-21.